Contents

Any words appearing in the main text in bold, **like this**, are explained in the Glossary.

KT-376-490

The Swiss Alps

Imagine walking along a path leading up a green valley in the Swiss Alps. It is a cool spring morning. The path is following a line of oak trees at the edge of a field, where cattle feed on the new grass. You are about to enter a forest. Beyond, there are steep slopes of grey rock and jagged mountain tops covered in snow.

Explorer's notes

Spring in the foothills:
- trees coming into leaf
- fresh cool air
- melting snow
- birds calling.

habitat *explorer*

Mountain Explorer

Greg Pyers

PROJECT LOAN

www.raintreepublishers.co.uk
Visit our website to find out more information about **Raintree** books.

To order:
 Phone 44 (0) 1865 888112
 Send a fax to 44 (0) 1865 314091
💻 Visit the Raintree Bookshop at **www.raintreepublishers.co.uk** to browse our catalogue and order online.

Published in 2004 by Heinemann Library
a division of Harcourt Education Australia,
18–22 Salmon Street, Port Melbourne Victoria 3207 Australia
(a division of Reed International Books Australia Pty Ltd,
ABN 70 001 002 357).
Visit the Heinemann Library website @
www.heinemannlibrary.com.au

First published in Great Britain by Raintree,
Halley Court, Jordan Hill, Oxford OX2 8EJ,
part of Harcourt Education.
Raintree is a registered trademark of Harcourt Education Ltd.

℞ A Reed Elsevier company

© Reed International Books Australia Pty Ltd 2004
First published in paperback in 2005

ISBN 1 74070 140 2 (hardback)
08 07 06 05 04
10 9 8 7 6 5 4 3 2 1

ISBN 1 84443 466 4 (paperback)
09 08 07 06 05
10 9 8 7 6 5 4 3 2 1

Editorial: Carmel Heron, Sandra Balonyi
Design: Stella Vassiliou, Marta White
Photo research: Legend Images, Wendy Duncan
Production: Tracey Jarrett
Map: Guy Holt

Typeset in Officina Sans 19/23 pt
Pre-press by Digital Imaging Group (DIG)
Printed in China by WKT Company Limited

National Library of Australia Cataloguing-in-Publication data:
Pyers, Greg.
    Mountain explorer.

    Bibliography.
    Includes index.
    For primary school students.
    ISBN 1 74070 140 2 (hardback)
    ISBN 1 84443 466 4 (paperback)

    1. Mountain ecology – Juvenile literature. I. Title.
      (Series : Pyers, Greg. Habitat explorer).

577.53

Acknowledgements
The publisher would like to thank the following for permission
to reproduce photographs:

APL/Corbis: p. 20; Auscape/John Shaw: p. 9, /Werner H. Muller-
Pater Arnold: p. 8, /Colin Monteath: p. 13, /Alan & Sandy Carey-
OSF: p. 18, /Jean-Paul Ferrero: p. 19; © Maurice Chatelain: p. 14;
Stefan Myers: pp. 7, 25; photolibrary.com: pp. 4, 6, 11, 12, 17,
21, 23, 24, 28, 29; Pomkin/Francedias.com/Daniel Ponsard: p. 27;
Christophe Sidamon-Presson: pp. 10, 15, 16, 22, 26.

Cover photograph of alpine ibexes reproduced with permission of
APL/Corbis/O. Alamany & E. Vicens.

Every attempt has been made to trace and acknowledge copyright.
Where an attempt has been unsuccessful, the publisher would be
pleased to hear from the copyright owner so any omission or error
can be rectified.

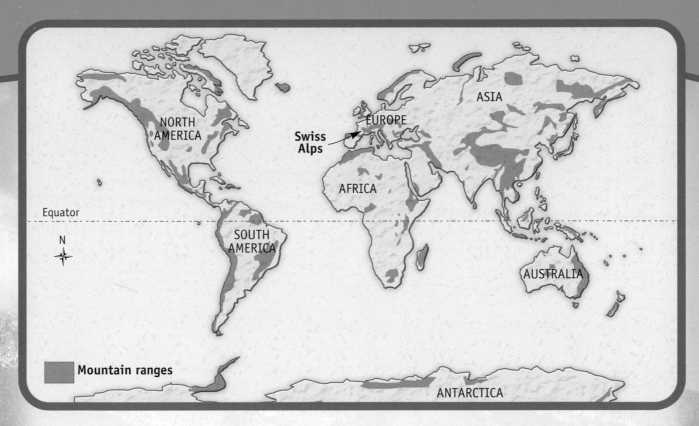

NORTH AMERICA

ASIA

EUROPE

Swiss Alps

AFRICA

Equator

N

SOUTH AMERICA

AUSTRALIA

Mountain ranges

ANTARCTICA

Mountain habitats

This exploration will take you on a journey from the mountain valley to a mountain peak. You will notice that in the mountains there are many different **habitats** – places where animals and plants live. You will also notice that each of these habitats is home to different kinds of plants and animals.

A mountain is usually part of a mountain range. This map shows the locations of the world's major mountain ranges.

Changing altitude

You have a map that shows the path ahead and the change in **altitude**. Altitude is how far above sea level you are.

Mountain valley

Signs of spring are all around. Though the air is cool, the sun is warm on your back. The rush of a mountain stream sounds through the trees. Higher up, snow that fell in winter is melting and filling the streams with more water than they will carry at any other time of year.

Glaciers

The valley you are in was formed by a **glacier** thousands of years ago. A glacier is a river of slow-moving ice that gouges out rock as it creeps downhill.

In spring, water gushes into the valleys from melting snow.

At the forest edge, two deer are grazing. They are beginning to lose their brown winter coats for the redder coats of summer. As the deer feed, they look and listen for signs of danger. By mid-spring the female will give birth. When the young deer, or fawn, is born, the mother will need to be especially alert for lynxes. These cats hunt fawns.

Deer graze at the forest edge in the mountain valley.

Explorer's notes

Description of valley:
- **altitude** 840 metres
- oak trees
- grassy fields
- forest
- gushing streams
- grazing roe deer.

A foothill forest

The path takes you through a forest of oak and beech trees. There are also a few chestnut and ash trees. Last autumn, these **deciduous broadleaf trees** shed their leaves. If they hadn't, the cold of winter would have frozen the leaves and the trees would have lost valuable water and **nutrients**. Now, new leaves are growing.

Explorer's notes

Trees at different altitudes

Altitude around 900 metres – broadleaf trees: oak, beech, chestnut, ash.

Altitude around 1200 metres – conifers: pine, fir, spruce.

Beech trees grow soft, new leaves in the warmth of spring.

8

Conifers

Moving further uphill, the path becomes steep. The trees here are mainly **evergreen conifers**, such as fir, Scots pine and spruce. Conifers are trees that produce their seeds in cones. At this **altitude**, winters are too cold for oaks and other broadleaf trees to grow.

The leaves of a white spruce tree are tough enough to survive a cold winter.

Adaptations

Animals and plants have features that help them to survive. These features are called **adaptations**. Important adaptations of conifers are their tough, needle-like leaves. A sticky substance called resin keeps the leaves from freezing solid in winter, and their needle shape prevents snow from settling too heavily on them.

Forest animals

In the **foliage** above, crested tits twitter as they hunt for insects and their **larvae**. Soon these birds will make their nests in tree hollows and raise their broods. There is a sudden flutter as a goshawk streaks through the trees in hot pursuit of a woodpigeon. On the ground, a ring ouzel is scratching at the pine needles to find grubs. This bird looks like a blackbird.

Viviparous lizards

Viviparous lizards emerge in spring from their winter shelters among the rocks. These lizards can survive at higher **altitudes** than other European lizards. Some have been seen at 2500 metres.

The crested tit eats insects, spiders and pine seeds.

This red squirrel is gnawing at a nut shell to reach the food inside.

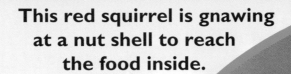

Squirrels

There are red squirrels in these trees. Their teeth can gnaw open pine cones to reach the seeds. Their long, sharp claws enable them to climb tree trunks quickly. This is important when pine martens are on the prowl. These weasel-like **predators** are excellent climbers and often eat squirrels.

Explorer's notes

Animals seen at altitude 1200 metres

Birds:
- goshawks
- woodpigeons
- ring ouzels
- crested tits.

Mammals:
- pine martens
- red squirrels
- polecats
- lynxes.

The tree line

The path cuts back and forth up the steep slope. The forest has been getting sparser and the trees shorter. The forest ends altogether at the **tree line**. The **altitude** is about 2200 metres. Beyond this point, the ground is too cold for trees to grow. The calling of forest birds is behind you now. The tree line marks the end of their **habitat**. It also marks the beginning of the habitat of birds of the high altitudes.

Bristlecone pines

Bristlecone pines of the dry mountains of southwestern USA are among the oldest living things on Earth. Some individual trees are 5000 years old.

The forest ends at the tree line.

Wildflowers

Out from under the cover of the trees, the light is brighter. With the snow cover gone, many wildflowers are blooming over the rocky ground. Butterflies are visiting these flowers to drink nectar, a sugary liquid produced by the flowers. As they go, these insects carry **pollen** from flower to flower. This is essential for the plants to form seeds before the autumn snowfalls.

These bright gentian flowers attract insects.

Explorer's notes

Wildflowers:
- bellflowers
- anemones
- gentians
- orchids
- wild tulips
- buttercups.

Alpine meadows

There are hoof prints and fresh animal droppings on the path. Ahead is a small **alpine** meadow covered in grass, and wildflowers such as orchids and pansies. Grazing here is a small herd of female **chamois** (pronounced 'sham-wah'). This herd has recently returned to high **altitude** after spending winter in the forest. As the weather warms and more snow melts, the herd will move even higher up the mountain.

Bighorn sheep

Bighorn sheep live high in the Rocky Mountains of North America. Like the chamois, adult males and females live for most of the year in separate herds. The males rejoin the females in autumn, at mating time.

In the spring, food is plentiful for this chamois herd.

Meadow birds

Many birds have arrived in the meadow. Alpine accentors, wheatears, rock buntings and water pipits spend winter in the shelter of the valleys. They move to these higher altitudes in spring to feed on berries, beetles, moths and grasshoppers. The birds will build their nests up here, either among the rocks or snug among the plants of the meadow.

The water pipit finds plenty of insects to eat in the meadow.

Explorer's notes

Butterflies of the alpine meadows:
- skippers
- peak whites
- apollos
- chequereds
- clouded yellows
- rock graylings
- ringlets.

Cliffs and screes

Cliffs rise steeply behind the **alpine** meadow. At their base there are **scree** slopes. These are formed by small stones that have tumbled down from above. The path leads you up and around the side of this unstable rubble. Wildflowers grow here and there in sheltered nooks.

On a cliff above, two wallcreepers are choosing a site on a rocky ledge to build their nest. Way above them, alpine swifts are streaking across the sky hunting insects.

A wallcreeper is able to climb steep cliff faces.

Explorer's notes

Wildflowers of cliffs and screes:
- alpine cabbages
- valerian
- creeping avens
- toadflax
- dwarf primulas
- saxifraga.

Ibex

The clatter of a falling stone echoes across the cliff. Something is moving. A dozen ibex are grazing the scattered mountain plants. These wild goats have sturdy hooves that grip the steep terrain. The females will give birth in a month or so. Before winter sets in, the herd will return to the **conifer** forest.

A male ibex uses his long horns to fight with rival males.

Animals of the Himalayas

High in the Himalayan Mountains of Asia live the serow, the takin, the markhors and the tahr. These plant-eating animals are all related to the ibex and chamois.

Hunters and Hunted

A large bird has appeared, gliding over the cliff top. It is a golden eagle. Through binoculars you can see the feather 'trousers' that keep its legs warm in the cold, high-**altitude** air. You watch it scanning the ground for **prey**, such as small **mammals**.

Explorer's notes

Mountain birds
of prey:
- golden eagles
- peregrine falcons
- kestrels
- eagle owls
- Tengmalm's owls.

In spring, a golden eagle may prey on young chamois and ibex.

You hear a sharp squeal and swing your binoculars downhill towards a patch of **alpine** meadow. A furry animal the size of a squirrel is still squealing. This animal is a marmot and these are its alarm calls. Other marmots stop grazing on the meadow plants and look for the danger. They see the eagle and, in a flash, they disappear into their burrows. Marmots feed over spring and summer to put on fat for the winter. They then go into their burrows and remain **dormant**, in a deep sleep, over winter. This is called **hibernation**.

Even when eating, a marmot stays alert.

The snowline

You have reached an **altitude** of 2600 metres. The temperature is 7° Celsius but the fresh breeze makes it feel much cooler. Uphill from you, the ground is almost completely covered in snow. This is the **snowline**. As more snow melts over the next month, the snowline will move up the mountain until the only snow left is at altitudes of 3000 metres or more.

Lichens

Lichens grow like colourful crusts on rocks. Lichens are living things made up of an **alga** and a **fungus** growing together in partnership.

Ptarmigan

A chicken-like bird suddenly pokes its head up from behind rocks below you. It is a ptarmigan (pronounced 'ta-mig'n'). With its white feathers, it is hard to see against the remaining drifts of snow. There are feathers on its feet and over its nostrils, which protect the bird from the cold. By summer, it will have grown a new speckled brown **plumage** that will provide **camouflage** among the rocks.

Explorer's notes

Ptarmigan food:
- crowberries
- wild strawberries
- bilberries
- cranberries
- buds
- worms
- insects.

A ptarmigan's white feathers help camouflage it in the snow.

Glaciers and bogs

The path leads you across a flat area. Moss grows among many of the rocks. Where water collects in **depressions**, plants grow thickly to form **alpine** bogs. All plants need oxygen to grow and most absorb oxygen through their roots. But the soil in these bogs is permanently waterlogged, which means that there is no air in it. So, the plants that grow here absorb oxygen through their stems.

This alpine lake is surrounded by a bog.

Explorer's notes

Dangers in the mountains:

- icy slopes
- **avalanches**
- falling rocks
- sudden drop in temperature.

Ahead is a wall of ice 20 metres high. This is the bottom end of a **glacier**, an ice river that is gouging out a valley as it creeps downhill. Here the glacier is melting and water gushes out from beneath the ice to begin a mountain stream.

This glacier is slowly carving out a mountain valley.

Lambert Glacier

The world's longest glacier is Lambert Glacier in the mountains of Antarctica.

The peaks

A final steep climb brings you to the top of a ridge, at an **altitude** of 3100 metres. Here is a world of grey rock and white snow. It is too cold for plants to grow. With no plants, few animals can live here either. In the quiet air, you realise that you are puffing. This is because your body needs oxygen but at this altitude oxygen levels are low.

Here, at an altitude of 3800 metres, the mountains are covered by snow all year.

Explorer's notes

Description at
3000 metres:
- icy winds
- slippery rocks
- bright reflections
from the snow
- distant views
- peaceful.

A chamois and her kid

In the shelter of a huge boulder on the slope below, you see a lone **chamois**. She bends down and through your binoculars you see that she is not alone at all. Her kid rises to its feet and stands next to her. Soon, the mother will lead her kid back to the herd.

Lammergeiers

Lammergeiers are vultures that search the mountains for carrion (dead animals). These birds feed on bone marrow. To reach the marrow, which is inside the bone, the lammergeier carries a bone aloft and lets it fall to smash on the rocks below.

This chamois and her kid will stay below the snow line, where there is food.

In the past

It is late afternoon. The weather can change fast on the mountain peaks so it is time to head back. There are no plants or animals to see now anyway, but the rocks catch your eye. There is limestone, a pale rock made of the skeletons of tiny sea creatures that lived millions of years ago. There is also granite, which was once **molten rock**. Forces deep within the Earth pushed the granite and limestone up to form the Alps. Where you are now standing was once beneath the sea.

Explorer's notes

Fossilised sea creatures in the limestone:

- ammonites
- trilobites
- brachiopods
- crinoids.

This limestone was formed beneath the sea millions of years ago. It is now more than three kilometres above sea level.

People in the Alps

Back down the mountainside, at 2300 metres, you see some rock paintings and carvings. These date from the Bronze Age, about 5000 years ago. Thousands of years before the people who made these paintings lived here, there were other people in these mountains. These were the Neanderthals. They hunted woolly mammoths and rhinoceroses.

This ancient rock carving is of a woolly mammoth.

Ice man

The body of a man who crossed the Alps 5000 years ago was discovered in 1991. Through all that time, the ice preserved his flesh.

Mountain future

The Swiss Alps are still being pushed up by the forces that created them. At the same time, wind and water, and the gouging of the **glaciers**, are wearing them down. This means that the Alps are constantly changing. But this change is slow. Other changes are much faster. One of these is a change in the mountain climate.

Mountain tourism

Tourism can be good and bad for the mountains. Good tourism protects natural places for people to enjoy. Bad tourism brings litter, too much traffic and inappropriate buildings.

Changing climate

The world is slowly warming up. As this happens, the mountain **habitats** are changing. For example, many of the 1800 glaciers in the Alps are already melting so fast that within 20 years they may disappear altogether. As the weather warms, trees may start to grow higher up the mountains. **Alpine** meadows may disappear as forests spread. Animals and plants that live in treeless places will lose their habitats.

Explorer's notes

Effects of warmer climate:

- changing habitats
- **extinction** of many plants and animals.

Find out for yourself

You may have an opportunity to visit mountains. Observe the different kinds of **habitats** you see. Observe the animals and plants you see in these places. What features do these animals and plants have that suit them to these mountain habitats?

Using the Internet

Explore the Internet to find out more about mountain habitats. Websites can change, so if the link below no longer works, don't worry. Use a kid-friendly search engine, such as www.yahooligans.com or www.internet4kids.com, and type in keywords such as 'mountain animals', or the name of a particular mountain range, animal or plant.

Website

http://www.mountains2002.org/kids.html
The International Year of Mountains website has links to sites about mountains of the world, including sites with fact sheets, games and videos.

Glossary

adaptation feature of an animal or plant that helps it to survive

alga (plural: algae) plant without roots or sap

alpine of the alps

altitude height above sea level

avalanche sudden fall of snow, mud or rock down a slope

broadleaf tree tree with broad leaves (e.g. oak, beech)

camouflage colours and patterns that help an animal to hide in its habitat

chamois goat-like animal that lives in mountains of Europe and Asia

conifer plant that produces seeds in cones (e.g. pine and spruce trees)

deciduous sheds leaves (usually in autumn)

depression wide, shallow hole in soil or rock

dormant inactive

evergreen retains leaves for the whole year

extinct when a type of living thing is no longer living

foliage leaves

fungus (plural: fungi) mushroom or toadstool

glacier river of ice that creeps slowly down a mountain valley

habitat place where an animal or a plant lives

hibernate become dormant over winter

larva (plural: larvae) young form of many animals

mammal animal that drinks its mother's milk when it is young

molten rock rock that has turned to liquid by heat

nutrient substance that provides nourishment

plumage feathers

pollen powdery material produced by the male part of a flower

predator animal that kills and eats other animals

prey animal that is killed and eaten by other animals

scree pile of loose stones that collects at the bottom of a cliff

snowline the altitude where snow melts

tree line the altitude above which no trees grow

Index